*L*ighthouses
of
*A*merica

Lighthouses of America

Text by

Bill Harris

CLB 2580
© 1991 Colour Library Books Ltd, Godalming, Surrey, England.
All rights reserved.
This 1991 edition published by Crescent Books,
distributed by Outlet Book Company Inc., a Random House Company,
225 Park Avenue South, New York, New York 10003.
Color reproduction by Scantrans Pte. Ltd., Singapore.
Printed and bound in Hong Kong.
ISBN 0 517 05313 6
8 7 6 5 4 3 2 1

CRESCENT BOOKS
NEW YORK

Portland Head Light, Cape Elizabeth, Maine. This, the oldest light in the state, was built in 1791.

Every now and then when the boss has been breathing down your neck all day and you get struck in noisy traffic trying to get home and away from it all, thoughts of a lonely seashore can be just the ticket to get your spirits back where they ought to be. And that thought sometimes leads to an even more romantic notion. Wouldn't life be close to perfect if you switched jobs and became a lighthouse keeper? Wouldn't it be terrific to spend all your time at the edge of the sea with the wind in your hair, the soothing sound of the surf in your ears and pristine vistas everywhere you look? There wouldn't be any boss looking over your shoulder, and the job would be satisfying because you'd be in the business of saving lives. And you could share your simple existence in the bosom of your family, safe from the outside world in a sturdy, cozy tower.

Spick-and-span Point Wilson Light in Washington State. This light was constructed in 1879 at the entrance to Puget Sound on the Quimper Peninsula. It was rebuilt in 1919.

Since the late 1930s you'd have to join the Coast Guard to make any part of such a dream a reality, and in the last several decades automation has been steadily making it a thing of the past. But many of the structures themselves are still out there calling you.

After the federal government took over the colonial lighthouses as one of its first official acts in 1789, the jobs were filled through political patronage, in many cases by men and women who apparently thought it must be the world's simplest task, with not much more involved than lighting the light when the sun went down and remembering to put it out again the morning. It had all the earmarks of a perfect sinecure, with nothing to do all day but carve scrimshaw and laugh with the gulls. The pay wasn't very good – as recently as 1900 it was only $600 a year – but the fringe benefits included free room and board and extra pay for firing a cannon or ringing a bell at regular intervals when the fog was too thick for the light to be seen. Many keepers also augmented their income by selling ships in bottles and other handicrafts to summer visitors. Some of the less scrupulous even managed to get rich by claiming salvage from shipwrecks they had been hired to prevent.

Of all the gifts from the sea, salvage has always been the one that men on shore dreamed most about. And it was one of the reasons why the government got into the lighthouse business in the first place. The first official light was built in 1716 on Little Brewster Island, at the entrance to Boston Harbor, where hundreds of vessels had been dashed on the rocky islands in thick fog. But before then, and for more than a century afterward, there were privately-

A Keweenan Peninsula light station, Michigan.

established beacon fires up and down the coast, even in Boston. Most of them were put there by well-meaning people who wanted to see their fathers and sons and neighbors get home safely. But they weren't charted, and because they were intended for local ships, masters of passing vessels were sometimes confused by them and ran aground. And that spawned a native American industry.

Because the cargo of grounded ships became the property of the people who removed it, some people began putting up false lights and even moving some that had become familiar. They usually went about their business on the darkest nights, when sailors had

difficulty making out the shoreline, which gave them the name "moon cussers." The lights were the seaman's only guide and when they were misplaced, they guided the ships directly onto reefs, where the waves would pull them apart. The moon cussers usually waited until morning to go out to the wreck, not so much because it was easier to work in daylight, but because the all-night pounding usually insured that all hands would be drowned. If any sailors were still alive in the morning, the land-based pirates killed them and then got on with their work with no worries about witnesses.

But in spite of local opposition, which was quite strong in places like

The lighthouse at Long Beach, California.

Bass Harbor Head Light, Mount Desert Island, Maine. This light, which was built in 1858, stands on the southwest point of Mount Desert Island. It is one of the most romantically situated lighthouses on the eastern seaboard.

Portsmouth, New Hampshire, where the offshore shoals were unusually treacherous, and in Key West, Florida, where the pickings were so good for pirates, the government went ahead with its determination to line the coast with proper seamarks. By the 1840s it was operating 256 lighthouses and 30 lightships. They served as life-saving devices, of course, but the authorities were just as interested in collecting every possible penny in customs duties, which were the government's main source of revenue in those days before income taxes. Pirates, land-based or otherwise, never paid them.

For the first decade or so, the administration of the lighthouses was handled directly by the President himself through the Treasury Department, but the responsibility finally came to rest in the office of the department's fifth auditor, a minor official who added keeping track of lighthouses to his job of keeping track of the country's money. Like any good bureaucrat, he shoved the responsibility down the line and put individual lights in control of local customs collectors, but he kept a tight control over his minions and personally approved every penny they spent. He was very pleased to be able to report after a dozen years of his stewardship that the typical American lighthouse cost half as much to operate as the ones along the English coast, and that his lightships were only draining a quarter as much from the public treasury. But professional seamen pointed out that there were four or five times as many shipwrecks off the American coast.

The master bookkeeper never pretended to know anything about nautical matters, but he was kept in charge of the lighthouses for nearly three decades before Congress decreed that each district along the Atlantic coast and the shores of the Great Lakes should

Heceta Head Lighthouse, which lies north of Florence in southern Oregon. Built in 1894, it is Oregon's most powerful beacon, having a one million candlepower light.

St. George Reef Light, which lies six miles out to sea just north of Crescent City in Northern California. It is one of the most exposed light stations on the Pacific Coast and several lighthouse keepers have been swept off the reef by high waves. In 1975 the light's service ceased and its lens was put on display in a museum in Battery Point Lighthouse near Crescent City.

15

Ned Point Light, Mattapoisett, Massachusetts.

Cape May Light on Cape May Point, New Jersey. This lighthouse, which was constructed in 1859, is the third to have been built on this site, the other two having been victims of cliff erosion.

have an experienced naval officer assigned to it. Their reports suggested that the reason American lighthouses weren't efficient was because they were usually misplaced, often badly built, in many cases not tall enough and in most cases poorly maintained. It took a few years, but Congress finally created a lighthouse board to set standards that included the hiring of more dedicated lighthouse keepers.

By then the job had already faded as one of the plums of political patronage. Before 1812, the lights they tended were pans of oil with wicks floating in them. They gave off fumes that burned the keeper's eyes, making it impossible to stay near them for more than a few minutes at a time, yet the oil in as many as thirty separate lamps needed to be replenished several times each night, and the smoke film on the windows needed to be wiped away even more often. It wasn't as though there was no alternative. European lighthouses were fitted with more efficient, smokeless lamps backed by reflectors for close to three decades before the Americans began installing them. But if the new technology was easier on the keeper's eyes, and the windows didn't have to be cleaned every hour or so, it brought a new chore, cleaning the reflectors.

The coming of dawn wasn't a signal that the lighthouse keeper could relax. Regulations required that the reflectors

should be polished, the lamps cleaned and refilled with fresh oil, the wicks replaced and the lantern windows washed, inside and out, before ten in the morning. To be sure, there was no boss standing by with pocket watch in hand, but one never knew when an inspector might drop around for a late breakfast. After breakfast, there was still more work to be done. The salt needed to be washed from the lantern platform, the stairways swept, the walls and floors cleaned and the brass polished. One early lighthouse keeper was well known for his ability to negotiate the circular stairway leading to the lantern without ever touching the railing. He was the one who had to wipe away the handprints.

The daily routine was broken by other chores, too. After lenses were introduced, they needed to be taken apart and thoroughly cleaned with alcohol once a month and polished every few months by hand with jewelers rouge. The lamp itself had to be replaced and

Point Arena Light, Northern California, replaced a light destroyed by the 1906 earthquake.

overhauled every two weeks. And when all that was accomplished, there were minor repairs to the structure that needed attending to, and the tower always needed painting.

Yet few lighthouse keepers ever spoke of their experiences without turning to the problems of loneliness and monotony. Not only were they in isolated locations, but if they were doing their jobs properly even ships at sea avoided them. A 19th-century keeper in Maine summed it up for all of them when he said, "the trouble with our life here is that we have too much time to think." He had his family around him, but very little contact with anyone else. His children had difficulty getting to school, and the youngsters living in many lighthouses very often didn't go at all. And a farmer's wife could consider herself a social butterfly in comparison to the keeper's wife.

The government wasn't insensitive to the problem, but it wasn't until 1876

Nubbles Light, Cape Neddick near York, Maine.

that it began doing something about it by establishing a library service to give lighthouse-bound families something to think about. About three dozen books were packed into a wooden case that could double as a bookshelf and rotated among light stations during quarterly inspections. No two collections were the same, and as keepers and their families dipped into them they noted the titles on a library card. The order of preference guided the selection of new titles, but by the time the box of books was replaced, every book had been read dozens of times. Over time, the surveys revealed that the classics, spicy novels and books of religious inspiration were preferred reading under a lighthouse lantern, but the most popular of all the choices was adventure tales of the sea.

The lighthouse keeper's family not only read together, but they worked together as well. And one of the sea adventures they never tired of telling and retelling was the story of young Abbie Burgess, daughter of the lighthouse keeper on Matinicus Rock, twenty-five miles off the coast of Maine. She was the oldest of five children who lived on the forty-acre island, and served as her father's assistant, which meant that she was in charge of the light on the rare occasions he went ashore. On one of those occasions in 1856, a violent storm hit the rock, sending waves crashing over the roof of their house, and Abbie rose to the occasion. The teenage girl evacuated her mother and sisters to the lighthouse tower and then raced upstairs to tend the lamps. The storm raged for an incredible four weeks, and the family's food supply nearly ran out, but the light never failed thanks to Abbie Burgess. History repeated itself less than a year later and she kept the light burning

Owl's Head Lighthouse, Maine.

Coquille River Light, Bandon Beach in southern Oregon. This lighthouse, which was built in 1896, lies within Bullards Beach State Park.

Prospect Harbor Point Light, Maine. This light is now part of a military base. It was built on the east side of the inner harbor in 1850 and rebuilt in 1891. The keeper's house is now used as a guest house by the base.

through another raging storm for two weeks. It must have been in her blood. When her father retired five years later, she married the son of his replacement and stayed on as assistant lighthouse keeper, a job she was obviously well-qualified to handle.

Not all of the moments of adventure and tales of bravery connected with lighthouse duty came from the sea. About forty years before the waves crashed over Abbie's house another assistant lighthouse keeper, John Thompson, turned the light at Cape Florida in Biscayne Bay into a fortress. The Seminole Indians had been threatening to attack the tower for weeks, and the regular keeper took the threat seriously enough

to remove himself and his family to the safety of Key West, leaving the job of tending the light to Thompson and a black man known only as Henry. When the attack finally came, the two men were able to make their way into the lighthouse tower, where they held off the Indians by firing muskets through its narrow windows.

They were able to keep the red men at a safe distance for most of the afternoon until a bullet grazed Thompson's head, and the Indians took advantage of the lull to charge the lighthouse again and torch the wooden door and the shutters covering the ground-level windows. In the meantime, their bullets had pierced the tanks of oil

The Lighthouse Museum at St. Michaels, on Chesapeake Bay, Maryland.

stored inside, and the ground floor quickly turned into an inferno. Thompson and Henry gathered up their muskets and a keg of powder and scrambled up the stairs, using an ax to chop away the stair treads behind them. By the time they got to the top, the door below had burned away and the draft through the opening turned the lighthouse into a chimney with flames roaring all the way up to the lantern. They were able to crawl out onto the outdoor platform, but the flames were so intense that the windows blew out and the two men, whose clothes were soaked in oil, were soon themselves on fire. And down below the well-armed Indians were waiting for them. Henry died quickly of his burns, and Thompson decided to follow him in death by tossing the keg of gunpowder down into the flames. But instead of blowing down the tower, the explosion only dampened the·fire for a few minutes and then the flames came back. The assistant keeper decided to go ahead with his suicide plan, but as he was poised at the rail to jump over the side he decided, for reasons even he couldn't explain, to turn back. Then, at almost the same moment, the fire burned itself out and a stiff breeze gave him some relief from his pain.

The Indians decided that both men must be dead by then, and after looting the keeper's house they set fire to it and escaped aboard the sloop that had been assigned to the light station. Thompson was indeed alive, but just barely so. As he later described his plight when the sun came up the next morning: "I was now almost as bad off as before, a burning fever on me, nothing to eat or drink, my feet shot to pieces, no clothes to cover me, a hot sun overhead, a dead man by my side, no friend near or any to expect, and placed seventy or eighty feet from the earth with no chance of getting down." He had resigned himself to what

Holland Harbor Light, known affectionately as "Big Red," in Michigan.

seemed an inevitable death when fate stepped in again. Late in the afternoon, a Navy schooner pulled up towing the light station's sloop, which the Indians had abandoned. If they had destroyed it instead, no one would have known about the siege of Cape Florida Light, at least not in time to save Thompson's life. But though help was in sight, he wasn't out of danger yet. The Navy men still had to devise a way to get him down from the top of the tower. They attached a line to a kite, but after several hours of trying to guide it into Thompson's hands they gave up in favor of attaching a line to a ramrod and firing it in his direction from a musket. Once the line was secure, some of the sailors climbed up and managed to lower the wounded man to the ground. He recovered and finally went back to duty, but not at Cape Florida. The light wasn't rebuilt for another ten years, and in a few more years vandals destroyed its lamps, keeping it dark for still another half-dozen years. The light was eventually abandoned completely, but reestablished in the 1970s. Ironically, even though the original tower had withstood the fire and the explosion of a barrel of gunpowder, it was discovered that the contractor who had been paid to build brick walls five feet thick had actually built a hollow-walled structure that probably couldn't have withstood the force of a hurricane. It was fairly easy to bamboozle the bureaucracy even then.

But when the Lighthouse Board was established the bureaucracy got more serious about setting standards for the lighthouse service. The dedication of men like John Thompson and his helper had provided inspiration for others, but it wasn't forgotten that they put their lives on the line because the regular keeper had decided not to. Under

Plymouth Light, Gurnet Point, Massachusetts.

Petit Manan Island Lighthouse, Maine. This lighthouse lies on a small island off Petit Manan Point. The tower, which stands at 123 feet above sea level, is the second highest in Maine. Built originally in 1817, it has since been rebuilt and frequently needs repair, as it is subject to the severest of storms in its exposed position.

the Board's reforms, new standards were established and most keepers rose through the ranks from such jobs as ordinary seamen aboard lightships. But in earlier times, an ability to read was about the only talent required, and sometimes even that rule was waived. There was no training period, but if a new recruit was lucky, the keeper he replaced might be on hand to explain how things worked. Otherwise, a government manual did the job. In fact, there were several, ranging from the straightforward "Lighthouse Establishment Instructions" to a masterpiece of governmentese called the "List of Illuminating Apparatuses, Fixtures and Supplies in General Use in

The U.S. Lighthouses, Lighted Beacons and Light-Vessels." And possibly to compensate for loneliness, every lighthouse keeper was provided with regularly updated lists of other installations in operation. The books and manuals dealt with every possible eventuality. They had detailed instructions for cleaning up oil spills, what clothes were least likely to scratch a reflector, even how to replace a door if the wind should blow it away. The books were necessarily quite heavy, and the Board thoughtfully also provided a summary of general instructions that could be posted inside the lantern, where they were probably needed most.

Hard as the government had tried,

a combination of quick turnover and general incompetence made the Lighthouse Service one of the least-respected of all the official agencies up until the time of the Civil War. It was said that as many ships were wrecked as their captains were trying to find a guiding light as were saved because one was there. But the personnel problem was only one of the things that put America years behind Britain and France in marking its harbors and danger spots. The real problem was politics.

In 1810, Captain Winslow Lewis revolutionized the operation of America's lighthouses when he demonstrated a new type of lamp at the Boston Light Station. It wasn't exactly a new idea, but an adaptation of one that had been illuminating French lighthouses for more than a quarter of a century. But it represented a leap forward for the Americans because its hollow wick and silver-plated reflector produced a light brighter and much cleaner than seven candles but used half the amount of oil. Government officials were impressed by the demonstration and the accountants were even more impressed by Lewis's offer to sell the government his patent, for a fee, of course, in exchange for a contract to refit all forty-nine of the federally-operated lighthouses with his new lamps. The accountants were also delighted to find that he was willing to make his fee for servicing the lights an

Warwick Neck Lighthouse, Rhode Island, which was built in 1939 and automated in 1986. It is made from cast iron and reinforced concrete, replacing an older structure of stone and wood.

amount equal to the value of half the oil saved by the use of his device, and his proposal to make the deal even sweeter by reducing the percentage to one-third if they renewed his seven-year contract which, of course, they did without the formality of competetive bidding. It was obvious that Mr. Lewis was more a sharp Yankee trader than an altruist. In the meantime, he had also secured a monopoly on the supply of whale oil used by all of the lighthouses in the country, and at the same time put himself in a position of recommending new lighthouse locations. By the time he died, one hundred new ones had been built. But for all that, Captain Lewis managed to delay any real improvements in America's lighthouses for another forty years.

In 1822, Frenchman Augustin Fresnel again revolutionized lighthouse technology when he developed a system that reflects and refracts light into a single beam, and intensifies it through a powerful magnifying glass at the center of what looks like a glass beehive. It used the same basic lamp as Winslow's collection of reflectors, but it was far superior. The Captain, on the other hand, had the complete respect of the accountants in charge, and when it was suggested that it might be a good idea to take a look at Fresnel's lens, Winslow recommended caution, especially in view of the fact that the biggest of the French beehives, twelve feet tall and six feet wide, cost $5,000, and that even the smallest was $2,000.

Finally, in 1838, Congress forced the issue and appropriated the funds to install a pair of Fresnel lenses in the lighthouses at Navesink, New Jersey. The auditor in charge may have been appalled at the cost, but he was

Eagle Harbor Light, Lake Superior, Michigan.

Jeffry Point Lighthouse, known affectionately as "the Little Red Lighthouse," stands directly underneath George Washington Bridge in New York City. It was the subject of a children's story, The Little Red Lighthouse and the Great Gray Bridge, *which sold two million copies. When it was proposed that the light be dismantled, a public outcry led to its permanent preservation. Although it no longer functions, its fame has ensured the little light many visitors.*

Assateague Light, Assateague Island, Virginia. When it was first built, the lighthouse was at the southern tip of Assateague, but the constant deposition of sand by the sea over the years has added much new land to that part of the island, leaving the light far inland. It is now part of the Chincoteague National Wildlife Refuge.

impressed by the result. Not only did he think the glass structures were beautiful, but he reported that "they appear to be the perfection of apparatus for lighthouse purposes, having in view only the superiority of the light, which is reported by pilots to be seen in clear weather a distance of forty miles." Then he went back to his ledger books, and thirteen years later only the Navesink Lights, Sankaty Head on Nantucket Island and Brandywine Screw Pile in the Delaware Bay were equipped with the new lenses, and each of them were installations forced by Congress. Obviously the time had come for a Congressional investigation. It ended with the creation of the Lighthouse Board and a policy

that required the conversion of all the American lighthouses to the new system, even though it could hardly be called new by then.

But there was no question of its superiority. The center of the dome-like collection of glass is a powerful circular magnifying glass with a set of prisms above and below it that refracts the light through the magnifier as a powerful beam of concentrated light. A steady beam is produced by a continuous fixed lens, or the light can be caused to flash by simply rotating panels around the outside of a series of bullseye lenses, with a mechanism powered by a falling weight very much like the ones that keep big clocks ticking. Colored glass was sometimes added to the outer panel to provide alternate flashes of red or green. But what made the Fresnel lens remarkable was that not a single photon of light was allowed to escape except through the concentrated beam. None was wasted in lighting the sky above or the lantern floor below. It seemed like perfection itself but, of course, nothing is so perfect it can't be improved. Toward the end of the nineteenth century the big beehives had gotten much bigger, and it was necessary to devise massive assemblies to hold them and the clockwork mechanisms that gave each lighthouse its own distinct personality. As more and more lighthouses were established, their flashing patterns needed to be more unique. A seamark flashing every five seconds could easily be confused with one whose beam appeared every ten seconds, which meant that groups of flashes neded to be produced to avoid confusion. The Minot's Ledge Light outside Boston Harbor, for instance, flashes in a pattern of one-four-three every thirty seconds, which beachgoers have long since interpreted as meaning "I love you." It was hardly what the planners had in mind, but no other light anywhere near it has a similar pattern.

Such innovations required faster rotations, which created a problem of friction on the roller bearings that not only promoted wear, but made it impossible to move the assembly, which weighed several tons, anywhere nearly fast enough to produce enough variety of occultation. The problem was solved at the end of the last century, when a French engineer suggested floating the whole assembly in liquid mercury. It reduced friction to the point that the whole thing could be moved with the

Rock of Ages Lighthouse, Isle Royale, Michigan.

touch of a finger, in spite of its weight, which meant that the lighthouse keeper didn't have to wind up the clockwork quite as often and almost never had to worry about replacing the bearings.

Many of the original Fresnel lenses are still giving good service after more than a hundred years, but the light source has changed considerably. Until the 1850s, only whale oil was considered good enough, but as its price kept climbing, the accountants kept crying for something better. Once again, it was the French who led the way. Their scientists had developed an oil from the seeds of a wild mustard plant that they claimed was just as efficient but only half the price of sperm oil. The Lighthouse Board quickly made the substitution, but before long the supply began to run out, a victim of its own economy. The price was so low that few farmers felt it was worth their while to grow wild mustard. But they did raise pigs, and it was discovered that lard made a good lamp fuel if it was pre-heated. It became the standard for another decade, until petroleum was discovered under the hills of Western Pennsylvania and kerosene became the fuel of choice for every lamp in America, including lighthouses. In the case of the latter, the liquid was forced under pressure into a heated chamber, where it was vaporized into a gas that burned with an intense white light. It was the brightest light yet harnessed by man and, just as important to America's pride, the technology was home-grown.

Then along came Mr. Edison and his wonderful electric light, and the days of the lighthouse keeper seemed numbered. There was no smoke so the lantern windows didn't have to be washed as often, and another inventor

Facing page: Split Rock Light, Lake Superior.

Point Bonita Light glows in the twilight across San Francisco Bay, California.

The light that must not fail.

had even come up with vertical carousel that automatically moved a fresh bulb into place when the old one began to dim. The only problem was that most lighthouses were far removed from power sources. Self-contained generators and storage batteries took care of that detail, but change was a long time coming, and it wasn't until after World War II that automation made most lighthouses obsolete and turned many of them into museums. But even the towers whose lights have been extinquished still stand as valuable day marks.

Mariners usually identify lighthouses by their shape during daylight hours, but because of their traditional appearance, many of the towers have been painted with distinctive horizontal stripes. In American lighthouses, red stripes are a sign that the structure is to the right of a major harbor and blue or black tells mariners that it is on the left side of the harbor entrance. In other places they are generally white, but visibility is usually enhanced with color, and in northern areas where winter snow and ice are likely to render a white tower virtually invisible, a vertical dark stripe solves the problem.

Most lighthouses have now been replaced, or at least augmented, by sophisticated electronic navigational devices, some of which even provide ships at sea with data from satellites in space. Radar and sonar help navigators steer clear of reefs and other underwater obstructions, but if the systems were foolproof we'd never have to worry about oil spills. Most of the dangers of the sea are not out in the briny deep, but close to shore. And because few fishermen and weekend sailors have an array of electronic devices on board, their lives still depend on lighthouses, and make it

Brown's Head Light, Vinalhaven, Maine.

highly unlikely that they'll ever completely outlive their usefulness.

Lightships, on the other hand, are already a thing of the past. Ironically, as a device for marking harbor entrances, floating lights are a relatively new invention. The first of them was launched in 1733 to mark the mudflats of the Thames Estuary in England, and it wasn't until nearly a century later that they were anchored outside New York and Boston harbors.

The first one at New York augmented the Sandy Hook Lighthouse and was appropriately also named Sandy Hook. A series of five different wooden-hulled lightships were on station there until 1908, when the Ambrose Channel was created and the position was moved for a new vessel named Ambrose. At the same time, a second lightship, Scotland, was placed at the southern entrance of the channel about five miles away. Scotland was retired in the 1940s and replaced by a massive buoy, and the last of the vessels named Ambrose went into the harbor to become a museum in 1967. She was the last lightship built in the United States, and when she went on station in 1952 Ambrose represented, as they say, the state of the art. She had what optical engineers call a catadioptric lens, the English translation of which is that it intensifies beams of light with mirrors. The light itself, suspended above the steel deck on a tower, was rated at 700,000 candlepower that could, when needed, be boosted to 2.5 million. The Coast Guard was proud of the fact that, if the earth were flat its light could easily be seen as far away as Philadelphia. It flashed in a pattern of three white pulses every eight seconds, as if to identify N.Y.C.

But lightships tended to move in

Wind Point Light, Lake Michigan, Wisconsin.

rough seas and there was always the danger of ramming by bigger vessels, and by the 1960s technology had advanced to the point of making it possible to replace them with stationary platforms of the type that were appearing all over the world to support offshore oil rigs. It's easy to speculate that oil drilling platforms led the way to improving lighthouse technology, but the fact is that the technology actually began with lighthouses.

The first offshore rig was built in 1930 off the coast of Sweden, and the Swedish government was so pleased with the result that it authorized ten more to replace its lightships, which had to be taken out of service in the winter because of ice buildup. World War II delayed the program and the refinement of the method of anchoring a prefabricated platform to the bottom of the sea. But the war also resulted in the destruction of many lighthouses that needed to be replaced, and the quickest method was the Swedish one. By building the components ashore and towing them out to sea, it was possible to have a seamark in place and operating in a matter of months, rather than the several years it traditionally took to build a masonry tower. The idea had even more merit because there were so many locations where a light is essential but a traditional tower can't be built. The platform that replaced the Ambrose Lightship is seven miles offshore in seventy-five feet of water, where winds are usually strong and tides move unusually fast. But the light station is up to the challenge.

It was built at Newport News, Virginia, and floated up the coast on barges, where it was raised up to the top of a framework of four steel legs anchored on piles driven to bedrock, almost 250 feet below the surface of the water and rising fourteen feet above it. The platform itself is two decks high, the lower deck housing fuel and water tanks and the one on top of it providing living and working space for the six Coast Guard personnel who run the station. The 70-foot roof doubles as a helicopter pad, but the crew, which works in two-week shifts relieved by one week of shore leave, comes and goes by boat, saving the choppers for emergencies and bad weather.

The station's light tower rising above its southeast corner houses a six-million candlepower beacon that can be seen flashing eighteen miles away. Unlike traditional lighthouse beacons, the light itself is a xenon-filled quartz tube and the time-honored sequence of three quick flashes is produced by a computer circuit. The station also has an electric fog signal that can be heard four miles away, and its radio beacon sends a strong homing signal for a distance of one hundred miles. The platform also contains an oceanographic laboratory that keeps track of such things as water temperature and current speed as well as salinity, wave heights and tide soundings. And its meteorological instruments are continuously reporting on atmospheric conditions. The whole thing, from the crew's television sets and washing machines to the obstruction lights that illuminate the entire platform, is powered by three Diesel generators, but the station also has enough storage batteries to get it through several days of full power should the generators fail.

The facility also takes the concept of lighthouses far beyond any tradition. It is the nerve center of a control pattern designed to prevent collisions not only among the more than 25,000 ships that pass it each year either entering or leaving the Port of New York, but among all the

Alkai Point Light on Puget Sound, Washington.

ships that come near the east coast of North America. The pattern establishes two-way shipping lanes for coastal traffic operating from the tangents of a circle extending seven miles out from Ambrose. One of them aims due east toward the Nantucket Light and the North Atlantic. A second follows the Hudson River Trench to the southeast toward South America and Africa, and a third due south toward Philadelphia and other ports along the American coast. Each of these super highways of the sea is about five miles wide, narrowing as they approach ports, and they are divided into inward- and outward-bound lanes by a buffer three miles wide.

The builders of the new breed of lighthouses are very proud of their advance testing to protect their structures from any hazard, from hurricane force winds to tidal waves to earthquakes, but nobody's taking any bets that any of them will beat the longevity record of the very first lighthouse ever built. The tower on the island of Pharos that was built in 300 BC marked the entrance to the harbor of Alexandria, Egypt, with an open fire some 450 feet in the air for more than 1,500 years before it was finally toppled by an earthquake. But even in its latter days, it was apparently none the worse for the wear of centuries. Not many years before it was toppled, a visitor wrote that, "... the whole is imperishable, although the waves of the sea continually break against its northern face." He said that its secret was in the fact that the stones were cemented together with melted lead. Not much more is known about the Pharos tower, except that its light could be seen almost thirty miles out at sea and the column of smoke from its fire could be seen even further away in the daylight hours. But it

Cape Florida Light, near Miami, Florida.

45

is generally believed that its basic design wasn't much different from the structures that lighted seacoasts in the eighteenth and nineteenth centuries.

Yet, though all kinds of seamark towers were built during the years between, the first lighthouse that could be considered a successor to the one at Pharos wasn't built until 1698. The tower on Eddystone Rock, fourteen miles off Plymouth, England, was the real grandfather of every lighthouse in the modern world. There wasn't a mariner anywhere who didn't agree that the underwater rocks it marked made passing through the English Channel the greatest challenge he could possibly face. But making them visible was an

even greater challenge. The authorities at Plymouth had been studying the problem for months when ship owner Henry Whitstanley, angered at losing two ships in a year, decided to take matters into his own hands and design and build his own tower. The only spot that could possibly support it was a jagged piece of rock that even seabirds avoided. Worse, it wasn't possible to work on the rock for more than three hours a day in the summer months if the weather was good, and the trip out to it from the mainland took six hours each way. But Whitstanley was a determined man. It took him and his men three years to anchor a granite platform to the sloping rock and build a wooden tower above it.

The restored Admiralty Head Lighthouse on Whidbey Island, Washington. Built in the early part of this century, the light contains the Fort Casey Interpretive Center, which displays exhibits on the history of the region's coastal forts. Fort Casey, which stands near the light, was once part of the coastal defense system.

Facing page: the light on Passage Island, which lies off the eastern tip of Isle Royale in Lake Superior. It marks the channel between the two islands which was heavily used when silver was discovered in the area in the late nineteenth century. The light was built in 1882.

A lighthouse keeper cleaning windows.

And when the entrepreneur personally lit the candles in its lantern on the night of November 14, 1698, he was the proudest man in Christendom. By the following spring, he had reason to be prouder still. It had been an unusually severe winter, but for the first time since the Norman invasion, no ship hit the underwater reefs. In fact, thanks to the Eddystone Light, not a single vessel was dashed against the rocks during six more winters. Then, on the night of November 26, 1703, the worst storm ever to hit Britain swept the light into the sea. Ironically, Whitstanley was on the rock that night and became one of the storm's victims, along with the lighthouse keeper and his family. Two nights later a merchant vessel on its way home from America scraped over the reef and went down with all hands.

It was obvious that the light needed to be replaced, but it took another three years before construction began on a tower that had been designed by another merchant and amateur architect, John Rudyerd. After studying the plan of the original tower, he concluded that one of its problems had been that it had been a polygon with flat surfaces that didn't deflect the wind. His solution was a slender curved tower, built like a ship. The lower half was of granite blocks bonded, as Pharos had been, with lead. Above it the outer wall was of oak timbers, alternating with courses of granite and held together with iron bands. And in the center of it all a timber mast rose from the base to the lantern. Rudyerd believed that by using wood, the tower would be less rigid than a stone structure and would be resilient enough to survive any storm. He was right. His lighthouse stood through the worst of winds for nearly fifty years. But it had a fatal flaw. In 1755 one of the two-pound candles tipped over and set fire to the lantern. The flames raced through the entire structure, and by noon the

Lighthouse Point Park Light in New Haven, Connecticut. This light no longer operates.

following day Eddystone Rock was bare once again.

The third Eddystone Light was built by an experienced engineer, John Smeaton, who studied the mistakes and the practical innovations of his predecessors and decided that, to be successful, a lighthouse needed to be massive and made entirely of stone. And with that theory came another giant step forward. He envisioned a tapering tower that resembled an oak tree, but made of stone and not wood. In order to make his tower strong and rigid, he decided that the granite blocks needed to be dovetailed together. Every one of the nearly 1,500 stones was cut in Plymouth, numbered and shipped out for assembly on the site. The entire process took more than three years, but workmen were actually on the rock less than a total of four months. It stood for 140 years and set a standard for building lighthouses that was never improved. It was replaced in 1882 by James Nicholas Douglas who followed Smeaton's principles, but designed a solid cylinder twice as high. He found out the hard way that dovetailed blocks was the right idea when his workmen began tearing the old structure down. The top half of Smeaton's Eddystone Light was taken back to Plymouth and reassembled, but the lower portion is still defying the waves out on the rock.

Eddystone's closest counterpart in America is the light above Minot's Ledge southeast of Boston Harbor. In the decade of the 1830s, more than forty vessels crashed into the rocks, which didn't show above the surface until three-quarters of the ebb tide, and even at extreme low tide were never more than three feet above it. When the wind was blowing from the northeast, ships

Marshall Point, Port Clyde Harbor, Maine.

A lone yacht passes Castle Hill Lighthouse in Newport, Rhode Island. This light was established in 1890 to direct ships through Narragansett Bay's East Channel. The owner of the land upon which it stands, Alexander Agassiz, donated the site to the government, but had cause to regret his generosity when a fog bell was also erected that struck a triple blow every ten seconds. Agassiz lived not far from the light and had the bell removed after listening to it for a year. Another, twice as big, replaced it though, so a compromise was reached by which a screen was placed around it to deflect the sound.

The Lakeside Lighthouse in Lakeside Park, one of the attractions of Fond du Lac, a resort at the southern end of Lake Winnebago, Wisconsin.

approaching Boston faced a constant danger of being driven onto the rocks. But even though Eddystone proved that it was possible to light such a hellish spot, the job wasn't tackled until 1847, when Captain W. H. Swift accepted the challenge. He chose to support the light with an iron skeleton that would offer less resistance to the sea, and suspended an iron box beneath the lantern to house the two keepers who would tend it, as well as providing storage space for their supplies. From an engineering standpoint, the tower was able to withstand any storm, but Swift hadn't taken the native Yankee ingenuity of the keepers into account. During their time on the rock, the men built a platform to

store the heavy barrels of water and oil and make them easier to get at when they needed them. They also attached a hawser to the lantern and anchored it securely to the underwater rocks, to provide them with an easy way to get up and down and to hoist oil up to the lantern. The platform increased the amount of surface buffeted by wind and waves and the heavy line was described as "having the same effect upon the lighthouse as would have been produced by a number of men pulling at a rope attached to the highest part of the structure with the design of pulling it down." Their labor-saving devices proved to be their undoing when a hurricane struck in 1851. When the storm

Tenants Harbor Light on South Island, Maine. This light is no longer functioning and is privately owned. It can be seen from the shore in the village of Tenant's Harbor.

Thousand Islands Light, New York State.

passed all that was left was a few twisted piles.

Its replacement, begun in 1855, was a 102-foot granite tower, following the example of Eddystone. The construction problems were the same, too. While workmen were cutting the foundations in the rock, a second crew constructed a scaffold above them, anchored to the holes that had been drilled for the earlier structure. It would serve as a support for a crane to move the stone blocks into place as well as a retreat for the workers when the waves began crashing over their heads. That part of the job took two summers, and then the real work began. Because the foundation was under water, it was necessary to pile sandbags around

the location for each stone and then bail the water out. Once the area was completely dry, a layer of cement was poured into it and the pre-marked stone placed over it. It was an agonizingly slow process. When the water level dropped too far for it to be removed with buckets, it had to be picked up with sponges. And a new, primitive cofferdam needed to be created for each stone. But the weather was good in the summer of 1858, and they were able to work for more than two hundred hours, which allowed the building of six courses. Because of the tight quarters and the nature of the work, the tower couldn't be made to flare at the bottom, as all lighthouses did until then, but the

A light on the Monterey Peninsula, California.

engineers compensated for it by binding the lower courses together with vertical iron rods extending into the rock below the base. They also fastened each of the thousand building blocks together with horizontal iron rods. It took them five years to finish the 102-foot tower, which was lighted in 1860. It was automated in 1947, and is still sending its well-known message of I Love You to ships at sea. Though there are no permanent residents on Minot's Ledge these days, some say that the old tower is haunted, and many old fishermen out of Boston steer a wide berth around it.

The ghosts first made their presence felt in the late 1860s, when the keeper went into the lantern one morning and

Split Rock Light on Lake Superior, Minnesota.

found the lenses and reflectors already brightly polished. When he went below to thank his assistant for doing the job, the man was still asleep. It happened again two weeks later, and though there were only two living persons on Minot's Ledge, neither of them had done the work. For years afterward, fishermen regularly noticed strange figures clinging to the ladder at the base of the tower and warning them to keep away. But the keeper and his assistant could usually be seen at the same time up in the lantern. Both men, and others who held the job, also reported hearing tapping sounds down at the base of the tower on dark nights. They were never able to find their source even though the tapping continued for decades.

It's easy to believe there may be ghosts in nearly every lighthouse. At least there are memories, and the romance they inspire is still very much with us. Not long ago, a retired lighthouse keeper who still thinks an ounce of tradition is worth several pounds of technology, went back to his old haunts. "Look at her," he said. "She's been here nearly a hundred years so far, think of that! The men who built her must have been very fine craftsmen, mustn't they, that she could have stood for so long against the sea. It's because those who designed her had the knowledge of the sea and the respect for it you've got to have before you start. You've got to have those to start off with. Otherwise the sea will treat you how you deserve."

Edgartown Harbor Light on Martha's Vineyard, Massachusetts. A light was established in 1828 on an island connected to the mainland by a little bridge, a favorite trysting place for the locals. The hurricane of 1938 destroyed both light and bridge, so the Coastguard thought to replace them with a steel tower. However, the locals petitioned against this and the authorities answered their pleas by using another nineteenth-century light brought from Ipswich, Massachusetts, in 1939.

Cape Elizabeth Light, near Two Lights State Park, Maine. This light was once one of a pair of lighthouses, the second, though, is now inactive, its top having been dismantled in 1924 when the government ruled that all lights should be converted into single beacons. Cape Elizabeth Light was originally built in 1829. Today it is automated and its beam, one of the strongest on this coast, can be seen for twenty-seven miles.

Marblehead Light on Lake Erie in Ohio. The Marblehead Peninsula is generally recognized to be the roughest point on the lake – hurricane-force storms are not unusual and the light was badly needed when it was built in 1821. Still in operation, it is the oldest on the Great Lakes.

Biloxi Lighthouse, Mississippi, shines out across the Gulf of Mexico. This light, built of cast iron in 1848, was dark throughout the Civil War because the Confederates were anxious not to give navigational help to Unionist shipping in the Gulf. In 1926 it was electrified and automated; today its tower is open to the public and boasts a display on its history.

The Cana Island Light, which lies northeast of Bailey's Harbor on the Door County Peninsula in Wisconsin. Built in 1851 and still in service, this light guides shipping through some of the most treacherous stretches of water to be navigated on Lake Superior.

Pickering Point Lighthouse on Winter Island, Massachusetts. This light was one of three established in 1870 to mark Salem harbor, which was the center of the China clipper ship trade at the time. All three were originally built for $30,000. Sadly, Pickering Point is now dark.

New London Ledge Light, Connecticut, which was established in 1910. When this light was automated in 1987 it was the last manned light station on Long Island Sound. It is reputed to be haunted by the ghost of a former keeper called Ernie, whose wife left him for the captain of the Block Island Ferry, driving her hapless husband to commit suicide by jumping from the fifty-eight-foot-high tower. The keeper's house is now an oceanographic school run by a private foundation.

Grays Harbor Light, the tallest lighthouse on the West Coast, which was built in 1897 near Aberdeen, Washington State. It stands 107 feet high and its third order lens sends a beam of light twenty-two miles out to sea.

Pemaquid Point Light was built in 1827 and stands on the western side of Muscongus Bay in Maine. Nearby stands a museum devoted to nautical and lighthouse items. The light is on a very exposed part of the coast and is frequently subject to the fiercest of storms; sadly, despite the light, several seamen have lost their lives after their ships were wrecked in the vicinity.

A small ray of hope, Destruction Island Light shines from the dark bulk of ominously named Destruction Island, Washington State. This light is one of three that work together. It lies a short distance to the north of Gray's Harbor Light, while the third in the team, North Head Light, is found to the south. Destruction Island Light was built in 1892 and is an iron tower clad with brick. Its light can be seen twenty-four miles out to sea.

The lighthouse on Fire Island, part of Long Island Sound, New York. Now designated a National Seashore, Fire Island is thought to have received its name for the fires that were lit on its shores during the nineteenth century to guide – or lure – ships attempting to navigate the waters of the Sound.

Point Betsie Light on Lake Michigan, Michigan. This light was built in 1858 near Crystal Lake and is important because it marks the turning point for several shipping lanes on Lake Michigan.

Grand Haven South Pierhead Inner Light in Michigan on the east side of Lake Michigan. This light was established in 1839 and rebuilt as a fifty-one-foot-high tower in 1905.

Old Yaquina Bay Lighthouse, which stands in Yaquina Bay State Park near Newport, Oregon.

The split rocks and bared roots that surround Eagle Harbor Light, Michigan, bear witness to the savagery of Lake Superior in winter.

Port Vicente Light was built in 1926 to mark the entrance to Los Angeles Harbor. Its tower stands 185 feet above sea level and its light is 600,000 candlepower, strong enough to pierce the fog for which this coast is famed.

New Cape Henry Light, Virginia, was completed in 1881, replacing the old lighthouse, which still stands nearby. The latter was the first light to be authorized and constructed by the United States government. It was built in 1791 in a spot close to where the first English settlers landed.

Trinidad Head Light in Northern California, north of Eureka. This diminutive tower, built in 1871, was designed to serve coastal vessels.

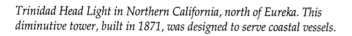

Battery Point Light, near Crescent City off the coast of Northern California, is found on a small island some twenty yards from the shore. Visitors may walk to it at low tide. Built in 1856 as a light and a keeper's house combined, today Battery Point houses a small museum.

Heceta Head Lighthouse lies within Siuslaw National Forest, Oregon.

Point Montara Light, which lies close to State Highway 1 on the Monterey Peninsula in Northern California. The light stands close to a youth hostel and is one of two vintage lighthouses to be seen from this highway, the other being Pigeon Point near Pescadero, which is the second tallest in the USA.

Nauset Beach Light in Eastham, Cape Cod, Massachusetts. The present steel tower was moved here from nearby Chatham in 1923, but a light was established here in 1839. The tower is forty-eight feet high and its 25,000-candlepower lamp is visible for seventeen miles. The light is at the center of Cape Cod National Seashore, very near to the Salt Pond Visitor Center.

Tillamook Rock Light, Oregon, which marked the approach to the Columbia River until 1957.

Bonita Point Light, whose beam can be seen from San Francisco's Golden Gate Bridge. The light marks the entrance to San Francisco Bay.

Little Annisquam Harbor Light on Wigwam Point in Gloucester, Massachusetts. It was built in 1801 at the entrance to the harbor.

The Old Lighthouse Museum at Stonington, Connecticut. This museum contains displays of ship models, whaling and fishing gear, swords, toys and Oriental artifacts. The sturdy, squat lighthouse was built in 1823.

Lynde Point Light at Old Saybrook, Connecticut, was established in 1803 at the entrance to the Connecticut River from Long Island Sound. It is a hazardous spot and steamboatmen often complained that mist rising from the salt marsh on the shore regularly obscured the light, so the tower was raised another twenty-five feet, making it eighty feet high. A fog bell, added in 1863, strikes every twelve seconds when weather conditions demand. Officially, the 1,000-watt lamp can be seen twelve miles away, but mariners have complained that they can't see it from as close as three miles.

Scituate Light in Massachusetts, a harbor light established in 1810, but
darkened when Minots Ledge was built because the two lights confused
mariners. The light is now the property of the Scituate Historical Society,
who open it to the public four times a year. In 1814, British ships headed
towards the harbor intending to invade, but the daughters of the lighthouse
keeper, named Abigail and Rebecca, hid in the trees playing fifes and drums,
which made the British think there was a garrison at Scituate, so they beat a
retreat. Whether or not this is true, Scituate was never attacked.

Sturgeon Bay Light in Sturgeon Bay, a town on Lake Michigan, Wisconsin.

The lighthouse dominates the landscape at Gay Head on Martha's Vineyard, Massachusetts.

North Head Light (above and above left) the southernmost light in a trio of lights that guards the entrance to Gray's Harbor, Washington State. The light lies on the Long Beach Peninsula and stands fifty feet high. It marks the spot where many fishermen catch their limit of silver and king salmon. The light is visible for an average of nineteen miles and was built in 1896.

Santa Cruz Light, which stands at the north end of California's Monterey Bay. The light was built in 1869 to mark the entrance to Santa Cruz harbor.

Northern California's lofty Pigeon Point Light, which lies west of San Jose.

The huge prism of Point Vicente Light, Los Angeles, which is one of the largest in the country. It is situated on the edge of the Palos Verdes Hills.

Cape Blanco Light, now disused, rusts on the Oregon coast in Cape Blanco State Park. This light lies close to Port Orford, the westernmost city in the contiguous United States.

The beautifully preserved light at Mystic Seaport, Connecticut. Mystic can boast numerous well-preserved or restored nineteenth-century buildings.

East Pierhead Light in Michigan City, Indiana. This lighthouse was established in 1838 to mark the location of the city on Lake Michigan.

One of two lights built at Navesink, New Jersey, in 1828. The lights resemble the towers of a castle, and climbing the north one provides views of Manhattan. The then brightest light in the world was installed in the south tower in 1938. It had a range of twenty-two miles. Today the lights are the centerpieces of Navesink Twin Lights State Park.

Brant Point Light, Nantucket, Massachusetts. The first Nantucket's ships beacon was built on Brant Point in 1746 to guide vessels into the Great Harbor. Since it was a fairly crude affair, consisting of lamps of highly inflammable whale oil on an elevated platform, the Brant Point beacon was burned many times before it was possible to make it a permanent structure.

With such seas as these on a comparatively calm day, it is possible to believe that waves of over a hundred feet are common along the Pacific coast. The light at Piedras Blancas on Point San Luis, close to San Simeon and William Hearst's Castle, in Southern California, remains vitally important. It stands 142 feet above the water and its 200,000-candlepower beacon is visible for eighteen miles.

Cape Hatteras Lighthouse, Hatteras Island, North Carolina. Guarding the Outer Banks, this light stands at 208 feet, making it the tallest such brick structure in the country. It was built in 1870 to warn shipping of the treacherous Diamond Shoals offshore, otherwise known as the "Graveyard of the Atlantic." Cape Hatteras Light is now closed to the public, though a nearby keeper's house has been made into a visitor center.

East Brother Lighthouse, more house than light seemingly, marks the entrance to San Pablo Bay, northeast of San Francisco, in Northern California. It was established in 1874.

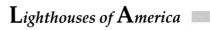

High tide at Blue Hill Bay Light on the central Maine coast. Built in 1935 on the tiny stretch of land known as Fly Island, this light marks an area of very shallow water. Indeed, the island's dimensions change considerably with the change of the tide; at low tide four or five times more land is seen.

As twilight brings to a close a cloudy New England day, clapboarded Gurnet Point Light starts to sparkle across Plymouth Bay, Massachusetts.

Heceta Head Light in northern Oregon, here looking the epitome of loneliness. No doubt the cries of the many seabirds present on the cliffs surrounding the light can be heard above the roar of the waves – often the only sounds of life a lighthouse keeper hears.

Burnt Coat Harbor Light, at the entrance of Burnt Coat Harbor at the southwest tip of Swan's Island, Maine. This light, which was built in 1872, is also known as Hockamock Head Light.

Indian Island Light, located at the eastern end of Rockport Harbor, Maine.
No longer a functioning light, this is now a private residence.

Point Montara Light in San Mateo County, where a savage, rock-strewn coastline and powerful offshore currents have claimed ships for centuries.

Maintenance of the light, including ensuring that all the beacon's windows are clean and undamaged after a storm, becomes routine for the lighthouse keeper, but no less vital for that.

Yerba Buena Island Light, which lies in the middle of San Francisco Bay. The light is situated at the northern tip of the island, the southern end being largely taken up by a massive support of the Bay Bridge.

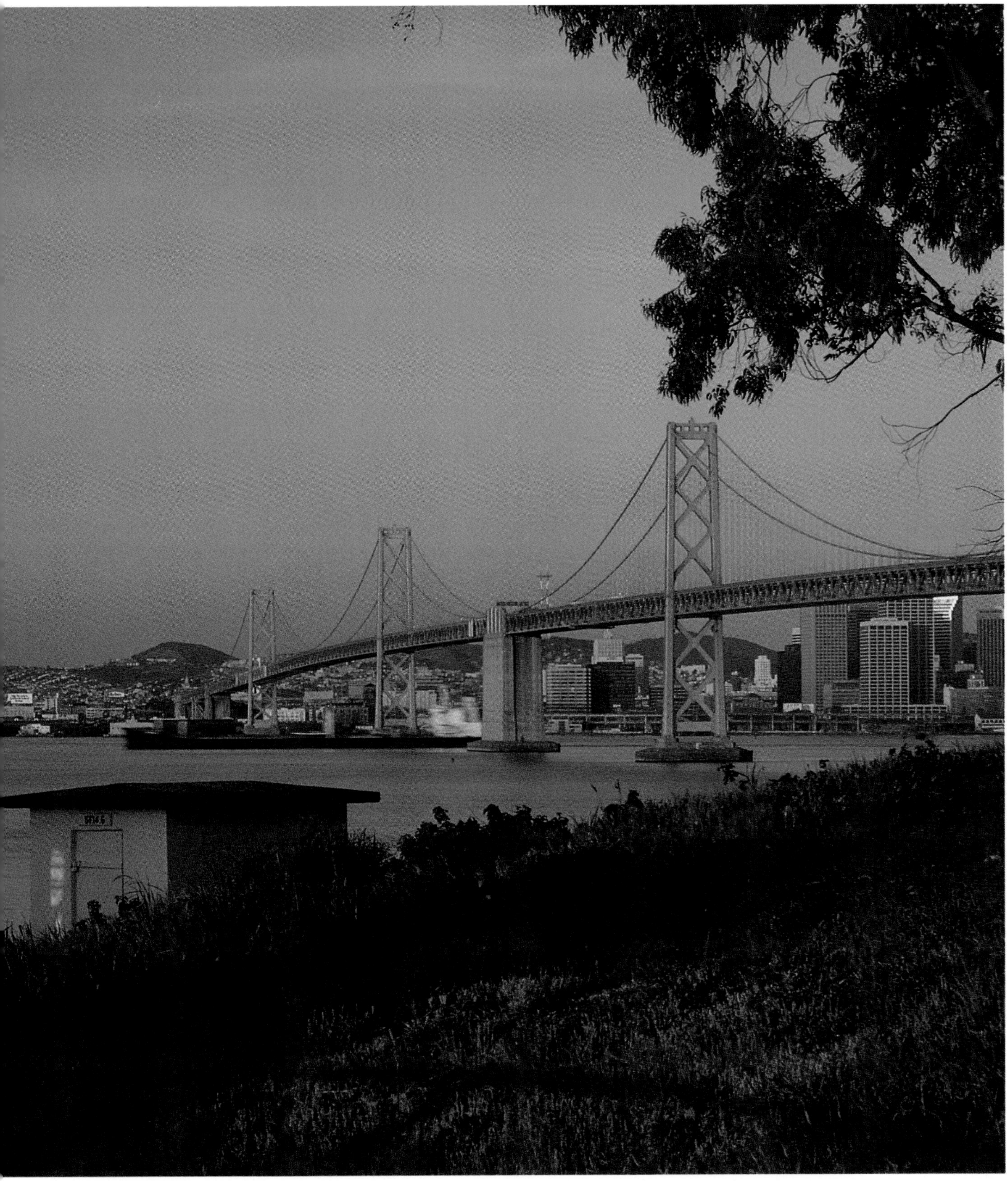

Gay Head Lighthouse, Martha's Vineyard.

Point Judith Light on Rhode Island lies at the point where the waters of Narragansett Bay and Long Island Sound meet. The first wooden tower was established in 1810. It was demolished by a hurricane in 1815 and was replaced the following year by the present thirty-five-foot-high stone tower. In 1938 an even greater hurricane destroyed a large part of the lighthouse's seawall and thirty feet of the beach in front of it, but the tower withstood the storm. There is also a Coastguard station on this site.

The New Long Light, Connecticut, which has been marking the mouth of the Thames River since 1760. The present light was built in 1801, a stone, octagonal tower eighty feet tall. When it was built the focal plane of its light was 111 feet above sea level, but today it is only eighty-six feet above the mean high water mark.

Currituck Beach Lighthouse in Corolla, North Carolina. This state is famed for its tall lights and Currituck is not a disappointment since it reaches 158 feet. A red brick light built on a hexagonal base, its glass lantern is surrounded by a circular walkway and railing. More remote than better known lights such as Hatteras, Currituck was built in 1875,

Sandy Hook Lighthouse lies in Sandy Hook State Park, New Jersey. Sandy Hook is a large sandbar jutting out towards New York Bay and this light stands at its tip. It was built in 1764 by New York merchants and is still used today, making it the oldest operational beacon in the New World.

Cape Meares Light, Oregon. The tower is only seventeen feet high, but its lens stands 232 feet above the sea.